50 POSITIVE AFFIRMATIONS

for Inner Strength and Self-Fulfillment

Sherry K. Ruth

To the best parents that anyone could ever hope to have, Anna and William Kopko, whose love and guidance allowed me to grow up independent, self-confident, and strong-willed, and whose support and encouragement taught me the value of hard work, persistence, and instilled in me the desire to go after whatever it was I wanted out of life.

And to my husband, soul mate and best friend, Bill Ruth, who, despite knowing what he was getting himself into, and that having an equal partnership was an absolute requirement, married me anyway. Thank you for the wonderful and fulfilling life we've had together as a team.

Suggestions For Utilizing This Book To Its Fullest Extent

This book is meant to be as much of a journal/workbook as it is an inspiration for achieving goals in your daily life. So, from a layout standpoint, the affirmations are always centered on the right (even numbered) pages, while the generalized, reinforcing statements that support the affirmations are always at the bottom of the left (odd numbered) pages. This is intentional so that you can have almost the entire left page to make your own notes to validate the affirmation for yourself or to jot down specific references for how that affirmation helped you cope with a particular issue. You can also use that space for anything you feel is relevant to helping you get the most benefit from the book. Please, PERSONALIZE IT as much as possible!

- Read each affirmation and the accompanying statement on the left facing page that goes with it, and take the time to think about the depth of its meaning (don't just read the words!), so you can get a FEEL for the flow and intent of the book.

- Decide if you would like to read one affirmation per day and focus on just that one to make it relevant for that day, or, if you'd rather reread all 50 everyday, and let the ones that have the most meaning for you on that particular day help you cope with whatever challenges you're facing in your life.

- On the left facing page, above the reinforcing statement, make notations to personalize the affirmation for use in your daily life. EX - To what current situation in my life can I apply this affirmation? Is there a visual in my mind's eye that can reinforce this affirmation? Is this affirmation relevant for me? Hopefully, you will eventually have multiple notations of successful incidences when use of that particular affirmation has made a positive difference in your life.

- Do some soul-searching and be honest with your evaluation of your usual mindset with regard to how you generally handle life's challenges; THEN you can realistically gain a better understanding of how using these positive affirmations can help you change your attitude so you can live a less negative, less stressful, and more satisfying life.

- ALWAYS phrase your notes and support statements from a positive standpoint, and in first person, present tense. EX. - what I WILL do, or what I DO want (NOT what I won't do or don't want)

- Learning to keep your mind in a positive frame takes practice - daily reinforcement of the affirmations will help to change your mindset from self-defeating negative, to self-assured positive. Pay attention to where your mind instinctively goes when a challenge arises - if it leans negative, immediately counter it with a supportive affirmation. Practice, practice, practice! Eventually, this will become an automatic habit.

- Some affirmations will be more meaningful and relevant for you based on your innate personality and current life situation- your need for specific affirmations will change over time as your experiences dictate.

- Regularly review and select a few affirmations that are the most appropriate at the moment for your life in general, or for a specific issue you are dealing with at any given time.

- Find one affirmation that is particularly meaningful to you and MAKE IT YOUR MANTRA, so that it automatically comes to the forefront of your thinking. Then LIVE by it!

- Use these affirmations to counter self-doubt whenever it creeps in.

- Make copies of your most inspiring affirmations and post them where you will see them on a regular basis. EX. - on the bathroom mirror (to start your day off with a good attitude), on the refrigerator, on the inside cover of your iPad, on your car's dashboard, on your workout clothes..... wherever you need a positive reminder to help you make the best decisions for yourself to keep your goals on track.

- Share this book with your kids to teach them how to become goal-oriented, self-assured, and able to counter life's negativity with positive self-reinforcement and vision.

- There are also blank pages at the end of the affirmations to use as additional journal space so you can record your goals and your own positive affirmations to support them (hopefully, this book is just the start for you....). Goals need to be written down and can relate to any aspect of daily life. EX. - relationships, athletics, job related, personal time, child rearing, financial management, retirement, weight loss...... anything that is an important part of your life. Include things like:

  - What is the goal?

  - What is my plan to achieve it?

  - List short term goals that must be achieved along the way - and a timeline for them.

  - What do I need to do on a daily basis to achieve each short term goal? Make a list and check each action off as you complete it to keep yourself focused and moving in the right direction.

  - Detail the longer term goals (that the shorter term goals will support) that must be achieved in order to cross the finish line for achieving the BIG goal.

REMEMBER -

"Winners see what they want",
Losers see what they want to avoid."

AND

"Every little bit I do today, pays off, big time, down the road!"

BECAUSE:

YOU ARE
AS STRONG
AS
YOU ARE
WILLING
TO MAKE
YOURSELF
BE

I have something I want to
accomplish everyday.

I WILL
LIVE
EACH DAY
WITH
PURPOSE

I can achieve anything I put my mind to.

I AM
FIERCE
IN MY
BELIEF
IN
MYSELF

Doing so is a basic survival skill.

I WILL
MANAGE STRESS
POSITIVELY
AND
PRODUCTIVELY

I trust my own judgment.

I AM CONFIDENT IN MY ABILITY TO MAKE GOOD DECISIONS

BECAUSE:

Your brain automatically moves
in the direction of your most
currently dominant thought.

I SEE
WHAT I
WANT TO
HAPPEN,
NOT
WHAT I
WANT TO
AVOID

A goal that is just verbalized is a wish;
A goal that is written down is a commitment.

I WILL
WRITE DOWN
MY GOALS
AND
ESTABLISH A
REALISTIC PLAN
TO
ACHIEVE THEM

BECAUSE:

I know I am a positive influence
on myself and others.

I
HIGHLY
VALUE
MY
SELF-WORTH

BECAUSE:

Things are often bigger in my own
head than they are in reality.

I WILL

KEEP A

HEALTHY

PERSPECTIVE

REGARDING

LIFE'S

CHALLENGES

I deserve the best.

I WILL
NEVER
JUST
"SETTLE"

I am a "mind over matter" person.

MY THINKING
CONTROLS
MY PERCEPTION
AND
MY REALITY

I will give purpose and pleasure to every day.

I WILL
SEE
EACH DAY
AS AN
ADVENTURE
AND A
CHALLENGE

My goal is to always be ahead of the game.

PROCRASTINATION
IS
NOT
MY
NATURE

Contentment is a necessary state of being.

I WILL
MAKE TIME
FOR ACTIVITIES
THAT
EASE MY MIND
AND
FUEL MY SOUL

| BECAUSE: |

It defines my reality.

PERCEPTION
IS
EVERYTHING

It makes my life feel fulfilled and meaningful.

I WILL
GLADLY
GIVE LOVE
AND
ACCEPT LOVE

BECAUSE:

They impede my path to
happiness and success.

I WILL ELIMINATE SELF-DESTRUCTIVE BEHAVIORS

.

BECASUE:

Negative energy is debilitating and destructive.

I WILL
SURROUND
MYSELF
WITH
POSITIVE
SUPPORT

It is a positive stress reliever and the closest thing we have to a "fountain of youth".

I WILL
MAKE EXERCISE
A PART OF MY
DAILY ROUTINE

I am willing to do whatever it takes
to live the life I want to live.

I AM
UNRELENTINGLY
PERSISTENT
IN THE
PURSUIT
OF MY
GOALS

| BECAUSE: |

Knowledge is power and that puts me in control.

I WILL
EXPLORE
ALL OF MY
OPTIONS
WITH AN
OPEN MIND

BECAUSE:

Wallflowers miss out on a lot.

LIFE
IS HOW
WE
MAKE IT,
NOT HOW
WE
TAKE IT

Mother Nature still knows best how to calm, restore, and rejuvenate.

I WILL
UTILIZE
NATURE
AS A
CENTERING
CORNERSTONE

Worrying about the "what ifs" is a direct path to limitation and self-doubt.

I WILL
LIMIT MY
WORRY
OVER THINGS
THAT ARE
OUT OF MY
CONTROL

Dealing with life's issues requires the understanding of different perspectives.

I WILL
SEEK HELP
AND ADVICE
WHEN
NECESSARY

"Me time" is important and I deserve it.

I WILL
ESTABLISH
A ROUTINE
THAT PROVIDES
OPPORTUNITIES
FOR
SELF-CARE

My nature is to never give in.

I
HAVE
TREMENDOUS
STRENGTH OF WILL

BECAUSE:

That is a life skill for happiness and success.

I WILL
MASTER
HEALTHY
AND
PRODUCTIVE
COPING SKILLS

BECAUSE:

What the brain believes, the body perceives and achieves.

I WILL
USE
POSITIVE
VISUALIZATIONS
TO ACHIEVE
MY GOALS

I want the most accurate information
in order to make the best decisions.

I WILL
TRUST,
BUT
DEFINITELY
VERIFY

Lack of preparedness causes
stress and uncertainty.

I WILL
ALWAYS
BE
PREPARED

Focus and attention to detail
make my goals achievable.

ONE
GOAL
AT
A
TIME

BECAUSE:

I am what I believe myself to be.

MY THOUGHTS,
MY SELF

I can't effectively take care of others
if I don't take care of myself.

I WILL MAKE SELF-CARE A PRIORITY

Knowing that I achieved the
goal is reward enough.

THE
ACCOMPLISHMENT
IS
THE
REWARD

I am strong-willed, determined, and
will never give up on myself.

I CAN

MAKE

MYSELF

DO

ANYTHING

BECAUSE:

I am secure in my knowledge of self.

CHIN UP!
CHEST OUT!
SMILE!

BECAUSE:

I take charge of my own life and
how I choose to live it.

I WILL
MAKE
THINGS HAPPEN,
NOT JUST
LET
THINGS HAPPEN

I have tremendous strength and a positive perspective.

I WILL
DEAL WITH IT -
PRODUCTIVELY!

BECAUSE:

I place no limits on myself.

I WILL
ELIMINATE
"CAN'T"
AND
"WON'T"
FROM MY
VOCABULARY

BECASE:

I decide where my life takes me.

I AM
IN
CONTROL

I like myself and I believe in me.

MY
SELF-TALK
WILL
ALWAYS BE
POSITIVE

Attitude determines dedication, which determines action, which determines success.

IT'S ALL
ABOUT
ATTITUDE

I must have the vision and belief in order to achieve the reality.

I WILL
"SEE IT"
AND
"BELIEVE IT"

I know I will never give up.

I AM
CONFIDENT
IN
MY ABILITY TO
OVERCOME
ANY
OBSTACLE

I will always fight for myself
and my best interests.

I WILL
BE
MY OWN
ADVOCATE

BECAUSE:

I carry myself with confidence,
intensity, and a sense of purpose.

MY
OUTER STRENGTH
WILL DEMONSTRATE
MY
INNER STRENGTH

Life's challenges make me
stronger and more capable.

I AM
RESILIENT
AND
IRREPRESSIBLE

That's how I am.

I WILL
FACE UNCERTAINTY
WITH
EMOTIONAL
STRENGTH,
TRUSTFUL PURPOSE,
AND
STRENGTH OF WILL

I know I can overcome any challenge.

I WILL
FEAR
NOTHING

I am!

BRING IT ON—
I'M READY!

I AM
AS STRONG AS
I AM
WILLING TO
MAKE MYSELF
BE

Positive adjectives to draw from to help with your self-image and positive visualizations:

Fierce	Indomitable
Relentless	Ruthless
Self-Confident	Willful
Persistent	Determined
Self-reliant	Purposeful
Strong	Mindful
Goal-oriented	Intelligent
Thoughtful	Influential
Optimistic	Realistic
Decisive	Masterful
Intuitive	Stubborn
Resolute	Inspirational
Creative	Resilient
Invincible	Headstrong
Feisty	Confident
Self-assured	Stoic
Spunky	Self-disciplined
Tough	Conscientious
Self-Motivated	Spirited

Use The Following Blank Pages As Your Own Personal Positivity Journal

Notes:

Notes:

Notes:

Notes:

Notes:

Notes:

Notes:

Notes:

Notes:

Notes:

Notes:

Notes:

Notes:

Notes:

Notes:

Notes:

Notes:

Notes:

Notes:

Notes:

Notes:

Notes:

Notes:

Notes:

Notes: